I KNOW OPPOSITES
CONCEPTOS CONTRARIOS

HOT AND COLD/
CALIENTE y FRÍO

Gini Holland

Reading consultant/Consultora de lectura: Susan Nations, M.Ed., author, literacy coach, consultant in literacy development/autora, tutora de alfabetización, consultora de desarrollo de la lectura

WEEKLY READER®
PUBLISHING

Please visit our web site at: www.garethstevens.com
For a free color catalog describing our list of high-quality books,
call 1-800-542-2595 (USA) or 1-800-387-3178 (Canada).

Library of Congress Cataloging-in-Publication Data available upon request from publisher.

ISBN: 978-0-8368-8304-6 (lib. bdg.)
ISBN: 978-0-8368-8309-1 (softcover)

This edition first published in 2008 by
Weekly Reader® Books
An imprint of Gareth Stevens Publishing
1 Reader's Digest Road
Pleasantville, NY 10570-7000 USA

Copyright © 2008 by Gareth Stevens, Inc.

Managing editor: Valerie J. Weber
Art direction: Tammy West
Graphic design: David Kowalski
Photo researcher: Diane Laska-Swanke
Production: Jessica Yanke
Spanish translation: Tatiana Acosta and Guillermo Gutiérrez

Picture credits: Cover (left), title page (left), p. 8 © Mary Kate Denny/PhotoEdit; cover (right),
title page (right), pp. 9, 16 (lower left) © Visuals Unlimited/CORBIS; pp. 4, 16 (upper left)
© Frank Siteman/PhotoEdit; pp. 5, 6, 7, 10, 12, 13 © Diane Laska-Swanke; pp. 11, 16
(upper right) © David Young-Wolff/PhotoEdit; pp. 14, 16 (lower right) © Corel; p. 15
© Theo Allofs/Zefa/CORBIS

Printed in the United States of America

1 2 3 4 5 6 7 8 9 11 10 09 08 07

Note to Educators and Parents

Reading is such an exciting adventure for young children! They are beginning to integrate their oral language skills with written language. To encourage children along the path to early literacy, books must be colorful, engaging, and interesting; they should invite the young reader to explore both the print and the pictures.

I Know Opposites is a series designed to help children read and learn about the key concept of opposites. In this series, young readers learn what makes things opposite each other by exploring familiar, fun examples of things that are *Alive and Not Alive*, *Soft and Hard*, *Light and Heavy*, and *Hot and Cold*.

Each book is specially designed to support the young reader in the reading process. The familiar topics are appealing to young children and invite them to read — and re-read — again and again. The full-color photographs and enhanced text further support the student during the reading process.

In addition to serving as wonderful picture books in schools, libraries, homes, and other places where children learn to love reading, these books are specifically intended to be read within an instructional guided reading group. This small group setting allows beginning readers to work with a fluent adult model as they make meaning from the text. After children develop fluency with the text and content, the book can be read independently. Children and adults alike will find these books supportive, engaging, and fun!

— Susan Nations, M.Ed., author, literacy coach, and consultant in literacy development

Nota para los maestros y los padres

¡Leer es una aventura tan emocionante para los niños pequeños! A esta edad están comenzando a integrar su manejo del lenguaje oral con el lenguaje escrito. Para animar a los niños en el camino de la lectura incipiente, los libros deben ser coloridos, estimulantes e interesantes; deben invitar a los jóvenes lectores a explorar la letra impresa y las ilustraciones.

Conceptos contrarios es una colección diseñada para ayudar a los jóvenes lectores a explorar y aprender la importante noción de conceptos contrarios. En esta colección, los jóvenes lectores aprenden mediante divertidos ejemplos a distinguir entre *vivo y no vivo*, *blando y duro*, *ligero y pesado* y *caliente y frío*.

Cada libro está especialmente diseñado para ayudar a los jóvenes lectores en el proceso de lectura. Los temas familiares llaman la atención de los niños y los invitan a leer una y otra vez. Las fotografías a todo color y el tamaño de la letra ayudan aún más al estudiante en el proceso de lectura.

Además de servir como maravillosos libros ilustrados en escuelas, bibliotecas, hogares y otros lugares donde los niños aprenden a amar la lectura, estos libros han sido especialmente concebidos para ser leídos en un grupo de lectura guiada. Este contexto permite que los lectores incipientes trabajen con un adulto que domina la lectura mientras van determinando el significado del texto. Una vez que los niños dominan el texto y el contenido, el libro puede ser leído de manera independiente. ¡Estos libros les resultarán útiles, estimulantes y divertidos a niños y a adultos por igual!

— Susan Nations, M.Ed., autora/tutora de alfabetización/consultora de desarrollo de la lectura

The fire is hot.

- - - - - - - - - - - - - -

El fuego está caliente.

The ice is cold.

- - - - - - - - - - - - - -

El hielo está frío.

The coffee is hot.

El café está caliente.

The juice is cold.
- - - - - - - - - - - - - - -
El jugo está frío.

The candle is hot.
- - - - - - - - - - - - - - -
La vela está caliente.

The snowflake is cold.

El copo de nieve
está frío.

The hotdog is hot.

- - - - - - - - - - - - -

La salchicha
está caliente.

The ice cream is cold.

El helado está frío.

The egg is hot.

El huevo está caliente.

The milk is cold.

- - - - - - - - - - - - - - -

La leche está fría.

The sun is hot.

El Sol está caliente.

The sea is cold.
- - - - - - - - - - - - - -
El mar está frío.

Which are hot?
¿Cuáles están calientes?

Which are cold?
¿Cuáles están fríos?